Horses and Ponies

Horse and Pony Care

Marion Curry

GARETH**STEVENS**
GS
PUBLISHING
A Member of the WRC Media Family of Companies

Please visit our Web site at: www.garethstevens.com
For a free color catalog describing Gareth Stevens Publishing's list of high-quality
books and multimedia programs, call 1-800-542-2595 (USA) or 1-800-387-3178 (Canada).
Gareth Stevens Publishing's fax: (414) 332-3567.

Library of Congress Cataloging-in-Publication Data

Curry, Marion, 1954-
    Horse and pony care / by Marion Curry. — North American ed.
      p. cm. — (Horses and ponies)
    Includes bibliographical references and index.
    ISBN-10: 0-8368-6833-1 — ISBN-13: 978-0-8368-6833-3 (lib. bdg.)
    1. Horses—Juvenile literature. 2. Ponies—Juvenile literature. I. Title.
  SF302.C87   2007
  636.1'083—dc22   2006002856

This North American edition first published in 2007 by
Gareth Stevens Publishing
A Member of the WRC Media Family of Companies
330 West Olive Street, Suite 100
Milwaukee, WI 53212 USA

Gareth Stevens managing editor: Valerie J. Weber
Gareth Stevens editor: Leifa Butrick
Gareth Stevens art director: Tammy West
Gareth Stevens designer: Kami M. Strunsee
Gareth Stevens production: Jessica Morris

Picture credits: Cover: © Bob Langrish; pp. 6, 19 Lisa Clayden; pp. 7, 12, 17 (bottom),
27 Shires Equestrian Products; p. 9 Chart Stables Ltd; pp. 13, 21, 29 © Bob Langrish; p. 14
Karl Norman; pp. 15, 16, 17 (top) E Jeffries and Sons Ltd; pp. 24, 26 Horseware Ireland.
All other images from Miles Kelly Archives, Corel, digitalvision, DigitalSTOCK, and PhotoDisc.

Printed in the United States of America

1 2 3 4 5 6 7 8 9 10 09 08 07 06

★ Cover Caption ★
A horse learns to trust the person who takes care of it.

Table of Contents

Words that appear in the glossary are printed in
boldface type the first time they appear in the text.

★ *Points* refers to specific parts or areas of a horse's body. *Condition* refers to the outward appearance of a horse. A shiny coat, clear eyes, clean nose, and ribs that can be felt but not seen all indicate good condition.

★ The withers are the highest point on a horse's back. They are found at the base of the mane, the thick hair growing on top of its neck.

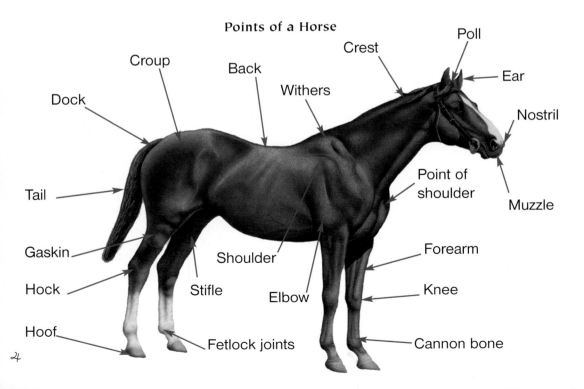

Points of a Horse

4

- ★ Hocks are **joints** on a horse's hind legs.

- ★ Horses have fetlock joints on all four legs. They are below the horse's knee on its front legs and below the hocks on its back legs.

Horses that work or travel on hard roads need metal shoes to protect their hooves. The outside layer of a hoof has no feeling, so nailing on shoes does not hurt a horse. The person who shoes horses is called a **farrier**.

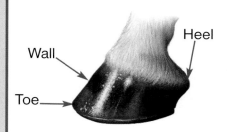

Outside of Hoof

Wall

Toe

Heel

- ★ The frog is the rubbery, wedge-shaped part on the underside of a horse's hoof. The frog helps soften the shock when a horse's hoof hits the ground.

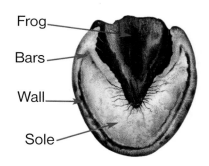

Bottom of Hoof

Frog

Bars

Wall

Sole

- ★ A horse's heels are at the back of its feet above the frog.

- ★ Laminitis is a painful foot condition that shuts off blood flow to the feet. A horse with laminitis will often stand on its heels to relieve the pain.

- ★ A horse often paws the ground with a front foot before rolling onto the ground. Pawing can also be a sign that the horse is sad or angry.

- ★ A horse needs new horseshoes every four to six weeks.

* A healthy horse has bright, clear eyes. It does not have any tears or other liquids running down its face. The ears should look lively. They should not droop or lie back along its head.

* A horse's normal temperature is 99.5 to 101.3 °Fahrenheit (37.5 to 38.5 °Celsius).

* When it is at rest, a horse usually takes between eight and fifteen breaths per minute.

Its pulse rate is normally thirty-five to forty-five beats per minute.

* Its coat should be springy and shiny, not dull.

* A healthy horse stands squarely on all four feet and shows no sign of swelling in its feet or legs.

* A horse should eat and drink normally. Its stomach should not make loud noises or be swollen.

* The tail should hang relaxed. A horse should not clamp its tail between its legs.

It is usually easy to see if a horse is in good health. It will appear relaxed and content as it **grazes** in the field.

By observing a horse's mood and its conduct, a person can make a good guess about its health. An interested expression suggests a horse is healthy and in good shape.

★ A healthy horse does not stand sadly at the back of its stall or away from its friends in the field. Grumpy behavior may be a sign that the horse is sick.

★ Sometimes worms live in a horse's system. A horse will get sick if the worms are not removed. A bad case of worms can give a horse terrible pains in its stomach.

★ Horses need regular **worming** throughout the year.

★ Horses also need **vaccinations**. Once a year, they should be vaccinated for horse diseases. Every three years, they should have shots to prevent rabies, a deadly disease.

★ When horses are kept in stables for a time to protect them from the cold, they may develop lung diseases. They are especially likely to get sick if their hay is full of dust.

A stable door should be tall enough for a horse to walk through easily without banging its head. The doorway in this picture is too low for the horse.

★ **Stables** shelter horses from very hot or very cold weather.

★ An average-sized horse stall in a stable is 12 by 12 feet (3.7 by 3.7 meters).

★ A stable should face away from the wind. The area in front of a stable should be paved. If it is not paved, the ground will quickly become muddy in wet weather.

★ A stable and its doors should be tall enough so horses do not bang their heads.

★ A stable needs good air flow so the air inside does not become stale.

★ An overhanging roof in front of a stable provides extra shade for the horses and protection from wind and rain.

★ Stable floors need to be very tough and should not be slippery. Concrete floors with rubber mats can be washed and **disinfected** easily.

Horses are well protected from rain and wind in this stable. The arrangement of the doors also allows the horses to see their companions.

★ Stables need regular cleaning. Someone must remove droppings and wet material daily, replace the water supply, and provide fresh bedding straw. Sometimes a stall needs to be disinfected.

★ Stable doors are usually divided in half. When the top part is open, the stabled horse can see out and get plenty of fresh air. The top edge of the bottom door usually has a metal strip to keep horses from chewing it. The doorway should be wide enough so horses can walk through it comfortably.

★ A horse will become bored if left in a stable for a long time. It may start behaving badly to show how it feels. It may walk around and around its stall, smashing stall walls or tipping over feeders and water buckets.

★ Horses have small stomachs for their size and need to eat many small meals. Horses will graze for most of the day in the fields. If horses do heavy work, their grass may not provide enough food to give them the energy they need. They may need extra food every day.

Apples and carrots can make a horse's feed ration tastier.

★ Food for horses falls into two basic categories: **fiber** foods, such as hay and grass, and mixtures of grains and nuts to provide energy.

★ Pasture grass is the most natural food for a horse. It contains a lot of fiber, which a horse needs in its **diet**.

★ A horse's diet must also contain the correct levels of vitamins and minerals.

★ Good hay should not appear dusty, smell bad, or have any visible plant growth on it. The best place to store hay is off the ground in a clean, dry area.

- All grain mixtures belong in rodent-proof containers to avoid attracting small animals and wasting food.

- A 1,000-pound (453-kilogram) horse will eat 2 to 5 pounds (1 to 2.26 kg) of grain mixture and 15 to 20 pounds (6.8 to 9 kg) of hay each day. It will drink 10 to 15 gallons (38 to 56 liters) of water.

- A horse drinks water by squeezing its lips together and using its tongue like a straw to suck up water.

- Water is important for sight and hearing. Tears bathe the eyes and liquids in the ears carry sound waves.

- A horse's muscles are 75 percent water, and its bones are 30 percent water.

- Clean water must always be available, either from a trough or from a tank that always keeps a pan full. Water containers should stand in frost-free areas so horses have good supplies of water during cold weather.

- Sudden changes to a horse's diet can upset its stomach. Changes should be gradual.

- During winter, horses often grow an extra layer of hair to keep them warm. Sometimes this hair hides the fact that a horse is too thin and needs more food. If the skin over a horse's ribs feels soft to the flat of a person's hand and is easy to move around, the horse is in good condition. If the ribs feel hard, the horse may need to get more to eat.

- One of the biggest costs of keeping a horse is buying its food. Giving a horse a well-balanced diet, however, is the best way to keep it healthy.

* Grooming is important for many reasons. It is a good way to keep a horse clean and observe its condition at the same time. Grooming also helps create a bond between a horse and its owner. A horse will learn to trust and obey the person who grooms it with kindness. Then the horse will allow this person to train it.

* The person who cares for a horse should be properly dressed. Gloves, sturdy boots, and riding hats protect this person.

* Grooming usually takes place outside so that old hair and dirt do not collect in the horse's stall. The groomer will need to put a **halter** and **leading rope** on the horse to tie it to the hitching post outside.

* The first step is to pick out any mud, stones, or dirt that may be stuck in the horse's feet.

* The next step is to brush any mud or dirt from the horse's coat. Brushing increases

Dandy Brush

Body Brush

Each kind of brush has a special use. In winter, a rubber **currycomb** and dandy brush will remove dried mud. During summer, a soft body brush is best. A metal curry-comb is good for cleaning brushes.

the blood flow in a horse's skin and helps keep its skin and coat healthy and clean.

★ A soft brush and sponge are good for cleaning the horse's face. It is best to remove the halter to clean its face. The groomer must put one arm around the horse's neck to keep the horse in place while it isn't wearing its halter. Then the groomer can clean the horse's face with the other hand. The areas where parts of the halter and bridle rest must be groomed thoroughly.

★ Massaging the skin with a thorough grooming removes dirt from the horse's coat and makes it look clean and shiny. Once its neck, body, and legs are finished, it is time to brush out its mane and tail.

A horse or pony is usually happy to be touched all over. It will stand still while being groomed.

★ A person should never sit or kneel down next to a horse while grooming it. It is better to squat in case the horse becomes startled and moves suddenly.

★ It is important not to groom a horse too much if it stays outdoors all the time. The natural oils in a horse's coat helps keep it warm and dry.

Bridles

★ The type of saddle and **bridle** horse owners choose depends on the kind of riding they will do. **English** riding started in Europe, and its rules go back many centuries. **Dressage** and show jumping follow the rules of English riding. Riders must dress and ride their horses correctly.

★ Western riding grew out of the way cowboys rode in the United States in the nineteenth century. It is more easygoing than English riding. Trail riding and rodeo stunts are big parts of western riding.

★ All riders use a bridle to control a horse's movement and direction. Pulling on both **reins**, for example, makes a horse lower its head, and that will make it stop walking forward.

The English bridle on this horse does not have all the silver decorations of a western bridle.

★ Most bridles are made of leather. The pieces of a bridle adjust easily to fit a horse's head. They come apart for cleaning.

★ Bridles contain a bit attached to the reins. A bit is the part of a bridle that fits into a horse's mouth. A bit does not rest on a horse's teeth. It hangs in a space called the bar — behind the front teeth and in front of the back teeth.

★ Riders must learn just how to pull the reins to give the horse directions. Tugging too hard on the reins pulls the bit against a horse's mouth. This motion can hurt the animal.

★ English bridles have a noseband, but western bridles usually do not. Western bridles usually have a lot of silver trim, and riders hold the reins loosely in one hand.

A double bridle has two metal bits and two sets of reins. It gives the rider very precise control. It is usually only used by experienced riders in top levels of dressage.

★ It is important to keep the bridle clean by regularly removing dirt and sweat and washing the bit in running water after use. Taking good care of the **tack** is part of watching out for a horse's safety and comfort. It also helps to make the gear last a long time.

★ Saddles are an important piece of **equestrian** tack. A good saddle fits both the horse and rider. The saddle carries the rider in the correct position without causing the horse any discomfort.

★ Most saddles are made of leather, but today some lighter plastic saddles are popular. Saddles come in many seat sizes to suit the rider. They also come in different styles, such as English, western, pony, jumping, and dressage.

★ It is important to clean a saddle regularly and check that the stitching is unbroken. If the stitching tears, lumps sometimes form underneath the saddle. These lumps could hurt a horse's back.

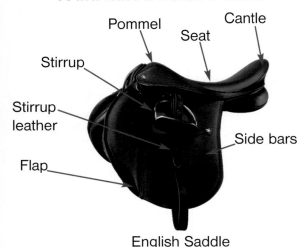

Pommel
Cantle
Seat
Stirrup
Stirrup leather
Side bars
Flap

English Saddle

Someone must check the stitching, the straps, and the leather flaps of a saddle regularly for wear and cracks.

★ *Fascinating Fact* ★

An English saddle has long side bars, no horn, a steel pommel and a leather seat. The saddle in this picture was designed in the seventeenth century.

A dressage saddle is slimmer than an English saddle. The leather flaps hang lower because dressage riders give their horses many commands with their legs.

Dressage Saddle

★ Horses often change shape as a result of exercise. A wise rider checks the fit of the saddle regularly.

★ **Girths** tie a saddle around the horse. They must not rub the horse or hurt the soft skin around its middle.

★ **Stirrup** leathers are the two leather loops that hang from a saddle. They hold the metal footrests, the stirrups, to support the rider's feet.

★ Western saddles are heavier than English saddles. They also have a broader seat and larger stirrups. They were built for a rider's comfort on long trips.

Western Saddle

The high horn in front on a western saddle was helpful in roping cattle.

19

- ★ COPD (chronic obstructive pulmonary disease) is an **allergy** usually caused by dust or seeds from very small plants. COPD makes it hard for a horse to breathe. A **veterinarian** should look at a horse with COPD. The vet usually suggests letting the horse stay outside as much as possible. It is also a good idea to keep its stable free of dust and to soak its hay in water. The tiny seeds swell in size when wet, and the horse is not likely to inhale them.

- ★ Leaving a horse standing in mud or a wet field or stable often causes thrush. This disease makes the bottom of the hoof smell bad. Keeping hooves clean can prevent it.

- ★ A horse can also get mud fever from standing in wet, muddy fields. It especially affects the back legs. Mud fever has many names including cracked heels, scratches, rain rot, greasy heel, mud rash, and dew poisoning.

- ★ A sore on the sole of the foot can make a horse **lame.** This common problem is often caused by small cuts that allow **germs** to enter the foot and infect it. A veterinarian can drain the sore to get rid of the infection.

- ★ Horses usually show that they are lame in one of two ways. If the horse is lame in a front leg, it will raise its head as the sore leg hits the ground. If it is lame in a back leg, it will **trot** unevenly. It might lean toward its good side and drag its sore hoof.

★ Tiny animals called ear mites often bother horses. A horse with ear mites might shake its head and try to scratch its ears.

★ Wartlike flakes in a horse's ears are usually harmless.

★ Colic is stomach pain. If a horse kicks at its stomach and tries to roll on the ground, it may have colic. Sometimes a horse will get swollen patches on its body from colic. A veterinarian must check a horse if it seems to have colic because the condition can kill it.

★ Lice often live on horses. If a horse tries to scratch the lice, it could make bald patches on its coat. If one horse has lice,

using its brush to groom another horse will give the second one lice. Powders and shampoos can treat the problem.

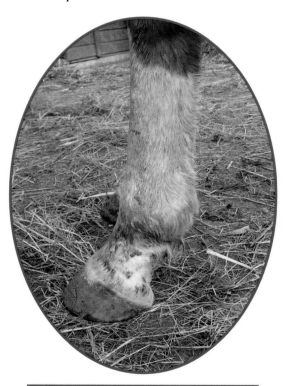

Mud fever affects a horse's heels and lower legs. It appears as sore, reddened, scabbed skin.

* Stress or boredom can make a horse behave badly. If a horse is kept in a stable alone for long periods of time, it will become unhappy. It may develop bad habits.

* Weaving is one bad habit. When a horse stands at an open stable door and swings its head from one side to another, it is weaving.

* Stall walking means refusing to settle down and walking around and around a stall.

* Cribbing is a habit of biting a solid object, such as a stall door, and gulping air. A cribbing horse can do a lot of harm to stables and fencing. It can also can wear down its teeth. Some horses swallow so much air they get colic.

* The solution to many of these problems is to put the horse outside more and give it the company of other horses.

* If a horse starts to misbehave when someone is riding it, the horse may be responding to pain.

* If a horse begins to **buck**, particularly when it is told to **canter**, the saddle may be hurting the horse. The saddle should be checked immediately.

* If a horse tries to avoid being saddled, the rider should check the saddle for lumps or tears. Massaging the horse's back might help, particularly for an older horse.

A **rearing** horse is dangerous. A rider can easily fall from the horse and be injured.

★ If a horse begins to shake its head, it may have a toothache. A professional horse dentist should examine its teeth.

★ Rushed or improper training. often causes a horse to rear or pull on its halter. If a horse does not understand what its owner wants it to do, it may become difficult to ride.

★ If all the causes of bad behavior have been checked, and the horse is still not behaving well, the horse may require further schooling.

★ A horse's rider may also benefit from further riding lessons to make sure he or she is giving the horse the right commands.

★ Most behavior problems can be solved if the owner identifies the cause of the problem and does something to fix it.

21

★ Horses have many ways of **communicating** with each other. They use their voices to neigh and whinny. They give each other small signs, such as flicking an ear to say they hear something coming. They give bigger signs, such as striking out with a leg or rearing. They stand in ways that seem to say, "I am boss" or, "I will do what you want."

★ Horse whispering is a way of using gestures and talking to a horse and in a manner that the horse naturally understands. People used to consider horse whispering magical.

★ By learning "horse language," it is possible to figure out a horse's problems. The first thing to understand is that a horse will run away from what looks like danger.

★ If a person walks straight up to a horse and looks it directly in the eye, the horse will see the person as an attacker. It may run away. The person should stand still and turn his or her eyes away. If the person dips one shoulder in the direction of the horse, the horse will see that it is a welcoming person. Then the horse might feel comfortable enough to approach. If the horse is not interested, the person can try to be accepted by walking in large arcs backward and forward toward the horse.

* Horses give basic signals of **submission**, such as smacking their lips, turning their ears toward their trainers, or dropping their heads down low. A horse that shows such signs does not want to go against the leader.

* Horses move other horses along by walking behind them and nudging them with their noses. A person can also move a horse by walking behind and slightly to the side of the horse.

* Horses have a natural fear of many things. People need to understand this if they want to train horses to trust their handlers and to believe that they will not be put in any real danger.

One horse will often form a stronger connection with another specific horse than with others in its field. This connection is called pair-bonding.

It is good to know right away if the price of a horse includes its tack.

history and ability. It is also important to consider its age, size, and personality. A responsible seller should be able to describe the horse's diet and produce veterinary and worming records.

★ Horses and ponies are bought and sold in many ways: from horse dealers, through advertisements, at auctions, and by buyers and sellers meeting.

★ Before buying a horse, it is important to find out as much as possible about the horse's

★ An animal's price varies according to its type, age, experience, and quality. A veterinarian should look over all horses and ponies before purchase. An exam can answer many questions about a horse's health and suitability.

★ Blood tests and X-rays can also be part of the exam procedure.

★ Horses take time to settle into new homes and may show unusual behaviors for the first weeks after a move. They might chew wood or start stall walking while they get used to their new surroundings.

★ Although many horses can and will live alone, they are herd animals and like company. Many people who buy a horse often buy a companion for it as well. Horses that are no longer suitable for riding, either because of age or lameness, are often advertised for sale as companion horses.

★ Anyone thinking of buying a horse should be ready to spend a lot of time with the horse. Horses need attention twice a day, every day of the year.

A companion pony might be relatively cheap to buy, but it will need the same kind of veterinary and farrier care as other horses.

★ When it is time to buy a horse, it is important to make sure its owner can load it into a trailer without problems so that the move is as gentle as possible. It may take several weeks of practice in advance to make this happen.

Long or short boots can be worn for general riding.

★ Someone riding for the first time at a riding school needs little special equipment. Regular, comfortable clothing is fine. Most riding schools are happy to provide safety hats for beginners.

★ A pair of strong boots with a small heel is necessary. Short or full-length leather boots give ankle support. A clearly defined heel keeps a rider's foot from slipping through the stirrup. Rubber rain boots, while ideal for working outside the stable, are not good for riding. They may get caught in the stirrups or slip through if they have no heel.

★ Riding clothes should be practical and neat and protect

A rider should always wear an approved safety hat for horseback riding. A velvet-covered hat is customary for competitions.

the rider in case of an accident. Riders should always wear protective hats that meet safety standards.

★ Jodhpurs or breeches are comfortable and practical. They protect the legs from being pinched or getting sore from rubbing against the saddle and stirrup leathers.

★ A body protector is a foam-filled vest that is worn over clothes. It protects a rider's back and chest in case he or she falls or is kicked. A body protector is a good investment.

★ A sweatshirt, heavy sweater, warm jacket, or raincoat are necessary for riding outdoors. Brightly colored vests, worn over outerwear, help make riders visible to others on the road or trail.

★ Gloves are very important, both to keep hands warm and to help the rider keep the reins in his or her hands.

★ Long hair should be neatly tied back.

★ Earrings or any other form of jewelry should not be part of a rider's outfit.

★ Riders who want to take part in competitive events, such as showing or jumping, will find dress codes for each sport that must be followed.

★ Beginning riders should check out riding schools by visiting them instead of simply setting up a lesson by phone.

★ When visiting riding schools, new customers should observe the condition of the stables and fields and how the animals look. They should find out what the school has to offer, such as indoor and outdoor arenas, floodlit areas, and barriers to jump.

★ Beginners will be given safety hats to wear during the first lesson. The instructors will find calm horses the right size for the riders. The first thing instructors show riders is how to get onto a horse.

★ During the lesson, an adult will probably walk alongside each rider with the horse on a leading rope to guide the horse.

★ Riders will learn how to approach a horse, how to mount, dismount, and sit correctly, and how to hold the reins.

★ New riders have to learn the basics of balance and stability in the saddle, so they do not injure the horses' mouths or backs.

★ Beginners will gain confidence as instructors introduce some movements just for fun. Riders might be told to "go around the world" on their ponies — taking their feet out of the stirrups and turning to face the ponies' tails. The instructors might ask the riders to lie back on their ponies and touch their tails.

★ Riders will feel the movement of the horses underneath them when they learn the rising trot and learn to "post," or rise in time with the horses' stride.

★ Later, when riders feel confident in the saddle and are able to control the speed and direction of the horse, the instructor will teach them to canter.

★ Gradually, riders develop a good, balanced seat and can handle the reins without hurting the horses' mouths. Riders need to be very good at the basics of controlling speed, turning, and stopping before learning to jump.

Glossary

allergy: a bad reaction, such as coughing or sneezing, to certain substances

bridle: a system of leather straps held together with metal that is put on a horse's head

buck: to spring into the air with arched back

canter: a quick run, slower than a gallop

communicating: making something known by signs or sounds

currycomb: a comb made with rows of teeth for cleaning a horse's coat

diet: food and drink

disinfected: cleaned of germs that can cause infections

dressage: an event in which a horse following orders moves precisely

English: a term describing a style of riding and type of saddle that originated in Europe; not just relating to England

equestrian: relating to horseback riding

farrier: a person who shoes horses

fiber: food like hay that is good for digestion but does not provide energy

germs: very small living creatures that make people or animals sick

girths: bands or straps for fastening a saddle

grazes: eats grasses and other plants

halter: leather straps for a horse's head

joints: the places where two bones meet

lame: unable to walk without pain

leading rope: a rope attached to the halter that is used for guiding a horse around

rearing: the act of a horse's standing on its back legs

reins: straps that riders use to control horses; part of a bridle

stables: horse barns containing stalls

stirrup: a pair of small rings attached to the saddle that support the feet of a rider

submission: behaving the way another person or animal wants

tack: equipment for a horse, such as saddle and bridle

trot: a brisk walk

vaccinations: shots to prevent disease

veterinarian: an animal doctor; also called vet

worming: a drug treatment to get rid of worms

For More Information

Books

Caring for Your Horse. Caring for Your Pet (series). Michelle Lomberg (Weigl Publishers)

Cherry Hill's Horse Care for Kids: Grooming, Feeding, Behavior, Stable & Pasture, Health Care, Handling & Safety, Enjoying. Cherry Hill (Storey Publishing)

Complete Book of Riding and Pony Care. Rosie Dickins, et al (Usborne Books)

Foal to Horse. Animals Growing Up (series). Jason Cooper (Rourke Publishers)

Horses: How to Choose and Care for a Horse. American Humane Pet Care Library (series). Laura S. Jeffrey (Enslow Publishers)

Horse & Pony Care. Kingfisher Riding Club (series). Sandy Ransford (Kingfisher)

Web Sites

Horsefun: The Homepage for Horselovers
horsefun.com/start.html
Quizzes, puzzles, stories, poems, brain teasers, and information about horse breeds and horse care

Pony Care
www.mda.state.mi.us/kids/countyfair/animals/ponies/care.html
Good advice on caring for a pony

Publisher's note to educators and parents: Our editors have carefully reviewed these Web sites to ensure that they are suitable for children. Many Web sites change frequently, however, and we cannot guarantee that a site's future contents will continue to meet our high standards of quality and educational value. Be advised that children should be closely supervised whenever they access the Internet.

Index